EARLY EXPLORERS OF TEXAS

Greg Roza

NEW YORK

Published in 2010 by The Rosen Publishing Group, Inc.
29 East 21st Street, New York, NY 10010

Book Design: Michael J. Flynn

Photo Credits: Cover, pp. 3, 4, 6, 8, 14, 18, 22, 24, 28, 30, 31, 32 (Texas emblem on all), cover (map), 3–32 (textured background), 9 (skull), back cover (Texas flag) Shutterstock.com; cover (Hernando de Soto and followers), pp. 4 (Native American), 11 (Cabeza de Vaca), 15 (Hernando de Soto), 22 (La Salle) MPI/Hulton Archive/Getty Images; pp. 5 (map), 17 (map), 20 (map), 25 (map), 27 (map) © GeoAtlas; pp. 7 (map; Seville, Spain), 8 (Cabeza de Vaca), 12–13 (map), 16 (Brazos River), 21 (Coronado expedition), 27 (marker) Wikipedia Commons; p. 14 (Hernando de Soto) Archive Photos/Hulton Archive/Getty Images; p. 19 (pueblo) George Eastman House/ Hulton Archive/Getty Images; p. 23 (The Murder of La Salle) Hulton Archive/Getty Images; p. 25 (salt mine) B. Anthony Stewart/National Geographic/Getty Images; p. 28 (Espada Mission) Alfred Eisenstaedt/ Time & Life Pictures/Getty Images.

Library of Congress Cataloging-in-Publication Data

Roza, Greg.
Early explorers of Texas / Greg Roza.
    p. cm. — (Spotlight on Texas)
Includes index.
ISBN 978-1-61532-454-5 (pbk.)
ISBN 978-1-61532-455-2 (6-pack)
ISBN 978-1-61532-489-7 (library binding)
1. Texas—Discovery and exploration—Juvenile literature. 2. Explorers—Texas—History—Juvenile literature. 3. Texas—History—To 1846—Juvenile literature. I. Title.
F389.R69 2010
976.4'01—dc22

2009031557

Manufactured in the United States of America

CPSIA Compliance Information: Batch # WW10RC: For further information contact Rosen Publishing, New York, New York at 1-800-237-9932.

CONTENTS

The First Explorers of Texas

The area today called Texas was once home to thousands of Native Americans. The first people arrived in the area more than 10,000 years ago. Native Americans of Texas did not share one common **culture**. There were more than twelve cultural groups. Some shared languages and beliefs that were much alike. Others were very different.

Native Americans lived in Texas for thousands of years before Europeans "discovered" it. They were really the first **explorers** of Texas. Some native tribes no longer exist, such as the Karankawas and Bidais. Many died in wars with Europeans or other tribes. Some died from illnesses the settlers brought with them. **Survivors** often moved away or joined other tribes.

AREAS OCCUPIED BY NATIVE AMERICANS IN TEXAS

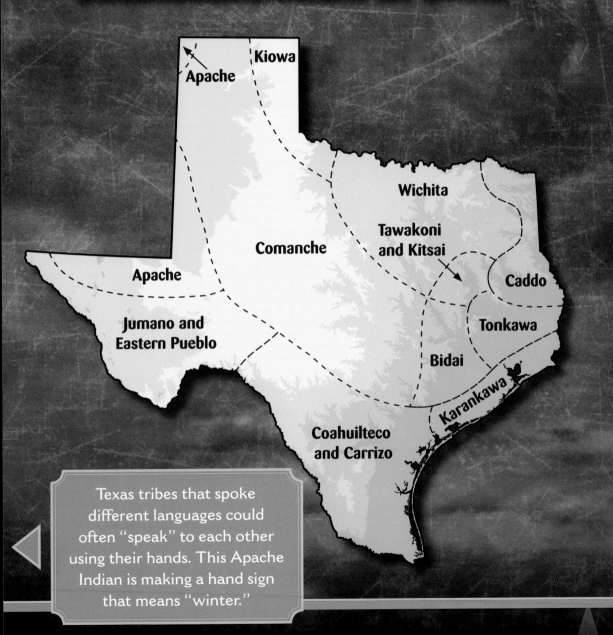

Apache

Kiowa

Wichita

Tawakoni and Kitsai

Comanche

Apache

Caddo

Jumano and Eastern Pueblo

Tonkawa

Bidai

Karankawa

Coahuilteco and Carrizo

Texas tribes that spoke different languages could often "speak" to each other using their hands. This Apache Indian is making a hand sign that means "winter."

ALONSO ÁLVAREZ DE PINEDA

In 1519, four Spanish ships left an **outpost** on the island of Jamaica in the Caribbean Sea. The **expedition** was led by Alonso Álvarez de Pineda. He was seeking a water **route** from the Gulf of Mexico to the Pacific Ocean. The ships sailed up the west coast of Florida and along the north coast of the Gulf of Mexico. Then they traveled down the coast of Texas and Mexico. They were stopped near Veracruz, Mexico, by Spanish explorer Hernán Cortés.

The Álvarez de Pineda expedition was important for several reasons. They discovered that Florida wasn't an island as Europeans once thought. They were the first Europeans to see the mouth of the Mississippi River. Most importantly, they were the first Europeans to map the Gulf Coast, including the coast of Texas.

The map made during the Álvarez de Pineda expedition is considered the first record in Texas history. Today it's in a museum in Seville, Spain.

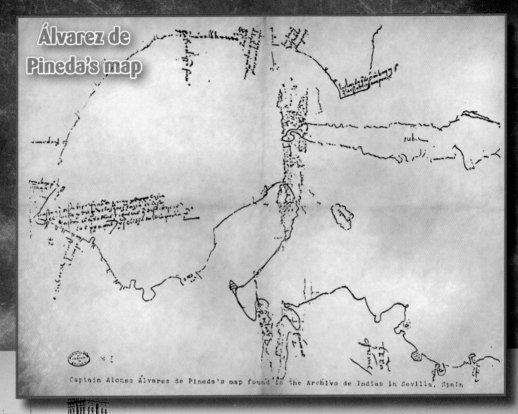

Álvarez de Pineda's map

Captain Alonso Álvares de Pineda's map found in the Archivo de Indias in Sevilla, Spain

Seville, Spain

ÁLVAR NÚÑEZ CABEZA DE VACA

In 1526, the Spanish king sent explorer Pánfilo de Narváez and more than 400 men to Florida. Narváez was ordered to **conquer** the Native Americans in the area. He was also meant to explore the land north of the Gulf of Mexico. A soldier named Álvar Núñez Cabeza de Vaca joined the expedition. Cabeza de Vaca's journey through Texas is one of the most exciting tales in American history. It's also one of the first historical accounts of Texas.

Little is known about Cabeza de Vaca's early life. We know about his travels because he wrote a book in 1537. It was titled *La Relación* (Spanish for "The Report").

What's in a Name?

Did you know that the term *Cabeza de Vaca* is Spanish for "cow's head"? This might sound strange. However, Álvar Núñez Cabeza de Vaca was actually very proud of it. An earlier family member earned the name after a Spanish battle in 1212. He marked a secret mountain pass with a cow's skull. The Spanish army saw the skull and used the pass to surprise their enemies. The Spanish king honored the man with the family name "Cabeza de Vaca."

In April 1528, the Narváez expedition landed in Florida near modern-day Tampa Bay. Narváez took 300 men, including Cabeza de Vaca, to explore the land and sent the ships away. Many men with Narváez died in Native American attacks or from lack of food. Separated from the ships, the men hoped to reach Spanish settlements in Cuba by **raft**. Hunger, thirst, and a bad storm killed most of the explorers. Only about eighty men lived to reach an island off the coast of eastern Texas. Narváez likely died in the storm.

At first, Native Americans welcomed the survivors. However, many Native Americans grew ill. They blamed the men of the expedition. Over the next 4 years, the Spanish suffered, too. Most of them died from illnesses, wounds, lack of food and water, and fights with Native Americans. However, Cabeza de Vaca survived.

Cabeza de Vaca became separated from the others and grew very ill. He later recovered. He became a trader between different Native American groups. He was even known as a powerful healer!

In time, Cabeza de Vaca met up with the last three survivors of the expedition, including an African slave named Estevanico. Mariame Indians captured them and made them slaves. They escaped in 1534. The four survivors traveled west, hoping to find a Spanish outpost.

Along the way, they met many Native Americans. Some told them stories of great riches to be found.

Historians aren't sure of the exact path they took. However, Cabeza de Vaca's records of the journey tell a great deal about the land and Native Americans of Texas and Mexico. The four men traveled down the coast of Texas. Next they traveled northwest, perhaps following the Rio Grande. They turned southwest toward the Pacific Ocean. Somewhere along the Pacific Coast, they met a group of Spanish soldiers. The soldiers guided them to Mexico City. In 1537, the men returned to Spain.

This map shows a possible route taken by Cabeza de Vaca after reaching Florida with the Narváez expedition.

Apalachee Bay

Tampa Bay

Florida

Atlantic Ocean

HERNANDO DE SOTO AND LUIS DE MOSCOSO ALVARADO

Before coming to North America, Spanish explorer Hernando de Soto found fame and fortune in South America. In the early 1530s, he joined an expedition to conquer the Inca. He returned to Spain a rich man.

De Soto heard Cabeza de Vaca's report of riches in North America. In 1538, he gathered a crew of about 600 men and set out for Florida. They spent the next 4 years exploring the southeastern United States. Historians argue about the route they took. However, they agree that de Soto died of a fever near the Mississippi River in what is now Arkansas. Before he died, de Soto made Luis de Moscoso Alvarado the new expedition leader.

Hernando de Soto

To avoid being attacked, de Soto told the local Native Americans that he was a god. When he died, the rest of the expedition hid his body. They worried the Native Americans would be angry about de Soto's trick.

artist's idea of de Soto expedition

Moscoso took over the de Soto expedition in June 1542. He decided to march west into Spanish territory rather than sail the Mississippi River. Some say the men started traveling west through Arkansas and then south until they came to Texas. Historians have tried to figure out their path using the Native American names in the expedition's report.

Brazos River

Moscoso likely made it as far as the Brazos River and perhaps farther into Mexico. The group had trouble **communicating** with local Native Americans. They also began running low on supplies. Moscoso led the men back to the Mississippi River. They built boats and sailed down the Mississippi River and along the Texas coast to Mexico.

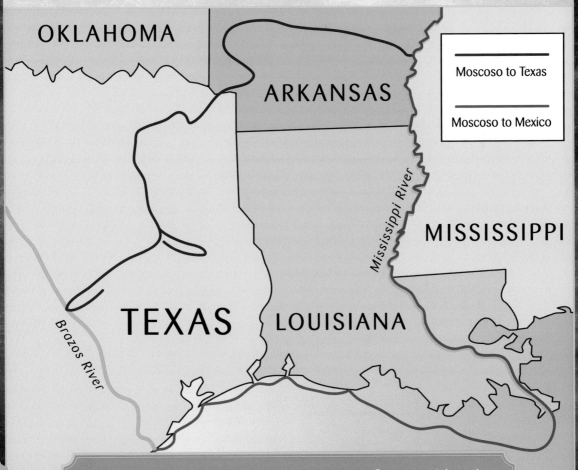

OKLAHOMA

ARKANSAS

MISSISSIPPI

Mississippi River

TEXAS   LOUISIANA

Brazos River

Moscoso to Texas

Moscoso to Mexico

The de Soto–Moscoso expedition was at first considered a failure. However, it provided knowledge about North America, Texas, and the people who lived there.

The Search for the Seven Cities of Gold

Cabeza de Vaca reported that Native Americans spoke of cities filled with riches. Some believed they were speaking of the **legendary** Seven Cities of Gold. In 1539, Spanish officials in Mexico City sent Marcos de Niza to look into Cabeza de Vaca's story. Estevanico went along as a guide.

Niza returned to Mexico City later that year. He claimed he had seen one of the cities of gold from a distance. However, Native Americans killed Estevanico and Niza ran away in fear. He said that the city, called Cíbola, was larger than Mexico City. He likely saw a Zuni **pueblo** located about 150 miles (240 km) west of the modern city of Albuquerque, New Mexico.

This photo shows the Zuni pueblo as it looked in 1873.

Spanish officials next chose explorer Francisco Vázquez de Coronado to find and conquer the Seven Cities of Gold. He set out from Mexico in April 1540 with about 1,000 men. Niza was their guide. In July 1540, Coronado conquered the Zuni settlement. He didn't find any riches.

Coronado continued to travel northeast, still looking for the Seven Cities. He also looked for another golden city called Quivira. The expedition crossed into northern Texas. This land was so flat and plain that some scouts became lost. Their journey ended north of the Arkansas River in Kansas. They never found the Seven Cities of Gold or Quivira. The expedition turned around in 1542 and went back to Mexico City.

In 1996, nails, arrowheads, and other supplies left behind by the Coronado expedition were found near Floydada, Texas. An artist's idea of the Coronado expedition is shown here.

René-Robert Cavelier, Sieur de La Salle

Between 1669 and 1682, French explorer René-Robert Cavelier, Sieur (Lord) de La Salle explored the land from the Great Lakes to the Gulf of Mexico. He claimed the Mississippi River and the surrounding area for France. In 1682, he named the area La Louisiane (Louisiana) in honor of King Louis XIV.

In 1684, La Salle led an expedition to the Gulf of Mexico. They landed in Matagorda Bay. In 1685, he set up Fort St. Louis—the first and only French settlement in Texas. It allowed France to claim a large part of the "New World." La Salle explored Texas between the Pecos and Trinity rivers. On March 19, 1687, he was killed by a member of his expedition near what is now Navasota, Texas.

René-Robert Cavelier,
Sieur de La Salle

Many historians think La Salle was killed because his crew thought he was a bad leader. Their ships had become lost on the journey to Matagorda Bay. They were also attacked by pirates.

ALONSO DE LEÓN

The Spanish government soon heard of La Salle's explorations along the Mississippi River and in Texas. They grew concerned about French settlements in Spanish territory. La Salle's settlement made Spain interested in setting up its own colonies.

The Spanish government sent explorer Alonso De León to remove the French settlers. De León made four expeditions to Texas between 1686 and 1689. When he finally reached Fort St. Louis in 1689, he found the settlement deserted.

Alonso De León became rich mining salt. Salt mining is still a part of the Texas economy today.

The Right Man for the Job

Alonso De León was born around 1640 in a section of Spanish territory in northeastern Mexico called Nuevo León. He was sent to school in Spain when he was 10. He spent a short time in the Spanish navy. De León then returned to his homeland to explore and make money in salt mining. Spanish officials thought his experience made him the best person to explore Spanish Texas and rid it of French settlers.

salt mine

Nuevo León

In 1687, De León became governor of the Spanish territory southwest of Texas called Coahuila (koh-ah-WEE-lah). In 1690, he helped found the first Spanish **mission** in east Texas. It was called San Francisco de los Tejas. De León also supported the idea of creating many more missions across Texas. Missions helped the Spanish spread their culture and faith to Native Americans in Texas. They also served as community centers for early colonists.

De León is remembered as an important **trailblazer** in New Spain. However, the paths along which he chose to create missions in Texas weren't new. He followed old Native American trails. In this way, De León helped found the Old San Antonio Road. Others continued to use De León's route. It became a well-marked trail through the frontier.

The Old San Antonio Road is known by many names, including King's Highway and Camino Real. A number of trails use these names. One of the main routes is shown here.

Arkansas

Louisiana

Natchitoches

TEXAS

Old San Antonio Road

Austin ☆

Houston

San Antonio

Guerrero

Gulf of Mexico

The End of Exploration

By the 1700s, the period of early exploration in Texas had ended. Spain soon established the first lasting settlements in Texas. By the late 1700s, there were about twenty-six Spanish missions in Texas. Although the missions started as Spanish outposts, early Texas settlements grew up around them. The first Texas colonists lived around the missions in San Antonio, Goliad, and Nacogdoches.

As interest in settling in Texas grew, the first American settlers arrived in eastern Texas. They found land perfect for farming and raising cattle. In time, others explored and settled central and western Texas as well. What do you think Texas would be like today if it weren't for the early explorers?

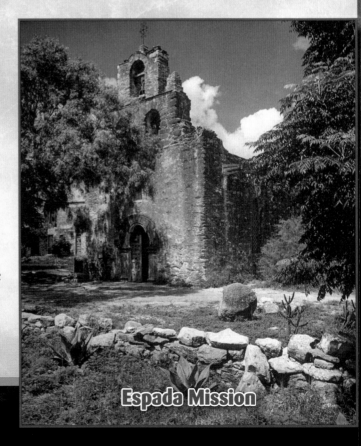

Espada Mission

EARLY EUROPEAN EXPLORATION IN TEXAS

1519 — Álvarez de Pineda begins exploration of Gulf Coast, including Texas.

1528 — Narváez expedition, including Cabeza de Vaca, lands in Florida.

1538 — De Soto's expedition sails to Florida.

1539 — Niza and Estevanico see a Zuni pueblo in New Mexico while searching for the Seven Cities of Gold.

1540 — Coronado begins search for the Seven Cities of Gold.

1542 — De Soto dies of a fever near the Mississippi River. Moscoso takes over the expedition and heads into Texas.

1684 — La Salle expedition lands in Matagorda Bay.

1685 — La Salle builds Fort St. Louis.

1689 — De León finds Fort St. Louis deserted.

1690 — De León helps found first Spanish mission in east Texas.

The San Francisco de la Espada Mission was one of the earliest Spanish missions. Parts were completed as early as 1745.

READER RESPONSE PROJECTS

- Choose one of the explorers in the book. Imagine that you are a soldier traveling with him as he explores Texas. Write a letter to someone telling them about the explorer and your travels. Include a map of the expedition.

- Choose two explorers in this book that you would like to know more about. Use this book, the Internet, and the library to find out facts about the two explorers. For each explorer, find the date he was born, the date he died, the nation of his birth, the total number of expeditions, his claim to fame, and any other interesting facts. Use the facts to make a chart or table comparing the two explorers. For an extra challenge, add one or two more explorers to the chart or table.

- List some ways Texas in the time of the explorers was different from Texas today. Then list some ways they are the same. Use your lists to draw two pictures showing how Texas in the past and Texas today are different or the same.

GLOSSARY

communicate (kuh-MYOO-nuh-kayt) To share facts or feelings.

conquer (KAHN-kuhr) To take control of a place by force.

culture (KUHL-chur) The beliefs, practices, and arts of a group of people.

expedition (ehk-spuh-DIH-shun) A journey with a purpose. Also, the group of people who make the journey.

explorer (ihk-SPLOHR-uhr) One who travels to a new place.

legendary (LEH-juhn-dehr-ee) Having to do with a story told many times, which is likely made up or only partly true.

mission (MIH-shun) A place where people teach their faith and way of life to others.

outpost (OWT-pohst) A military base in an area far away from the country that set it up.

pueblo (PWEH-bloh) A Native American village with square, connected homes made of stone or clay bricks.

raft (RAFT) A kind of flat boat.

route (ROOT) A path someone follows.

survivor (suhr-VY-vuhr) Someone who lived through a dangerous event.

trailblazer (TRAYL-blay-zuhr) Someone who makes a new path through a wilderness.

INDEX

Due to the changing nature of Internet links, the Rosen Publishing Group, Inc., has developed an online list of Web sites related to the subject of this book. This site is updated regularly. Please use this link to access the list: **http://www.rcbmlinks.com/sot/extex/**